This igloo book belongs to:

....

....

igloobooks

Published in 2015
by Igloo Books Ltd
Cottage Farm
Sywell
NN6 0BJ
www.igloobooks.com

LEO002 0915
4 6 8 10 9 7 5
ISBN 978-1-78343-829-7

Illustrated by James Newman Gray
Additional colour by Nigel Chilvers
Written by Melanie Joyce

Printed and manufactured in China

Melanie Joyce

James Newman Gray

The Magical Toy Box

igloobooks

The clock struck twelve at Lucy's house and she was fast asleep.
Across the moonlit bedroom floor, shadows began to creep.

A sound came from the toybox.
The lid creaked and opened wide.
"It's time to play," whispered Teddy, to all the toys inside.

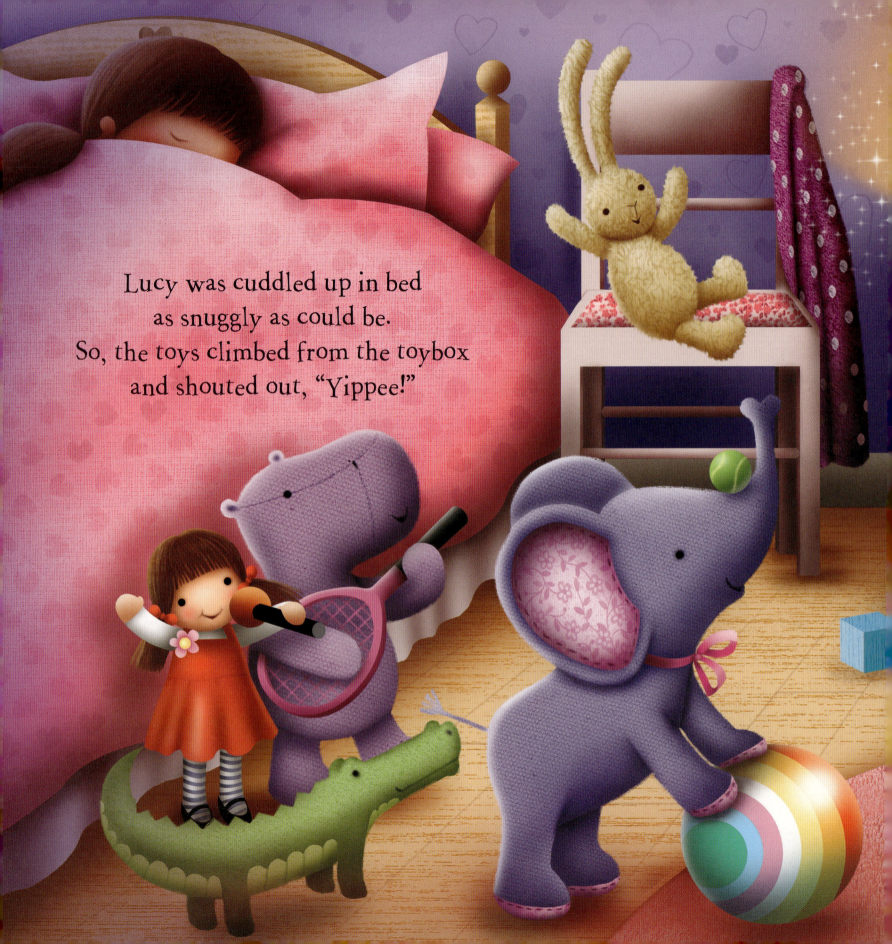

Lucy was cuddled up in bed
as snuggly as could be.
So, the toys climbed from the toybox
and shouted out, "Yippee!"

"Shh, now, don't wake Lucy.
Be quiet, you naughty toys.
Bring the disco ball," said Teddy.
"Don't make too much noise."

"Woof-woof," said Puppy, wagging his tail,
sniffing under the bed.
He pulled out the lid of an old board game.
"I've got an **idea**," he said.

The toys crept into the hall,
so quietly, on tiptoe.
They climbed on board and Puppy said,

"Hold on tight.

Let's go!"

Who

oosh!

They slid down the stairs,
with a bumpety-bump.
Everyone landed,
thumpety-thump.

Creeeak!

Teddy opened the living room door.
"Come on," he said, "Let's go."
"I've found the perfect place
for a brilliant toy disco."

Soon, the disco ball was glittering.
It swirled and whirled around.

"Everybody dance!" cried Teddy.
"Dig that disco sound!"

Hippo wiggled and Monkey giggled,
as all the toys began to bop.

Singing along, as he danced to the song,
Bunny went hippety-hop!

"Time for a break!" cried Teddy,
as his hungry tummy rumbled.
Into the kitchen, to find some food,
the happy toys all tumbled.

They piled their plates with cookies and cake
and tasty things to eat.

Monkey munched, Croc went crunch
and they gobbled up every treat.

At last the toys were really full
and couldn't eat one bite more.
It was time to tidy up, so
Bunny swept the floor.

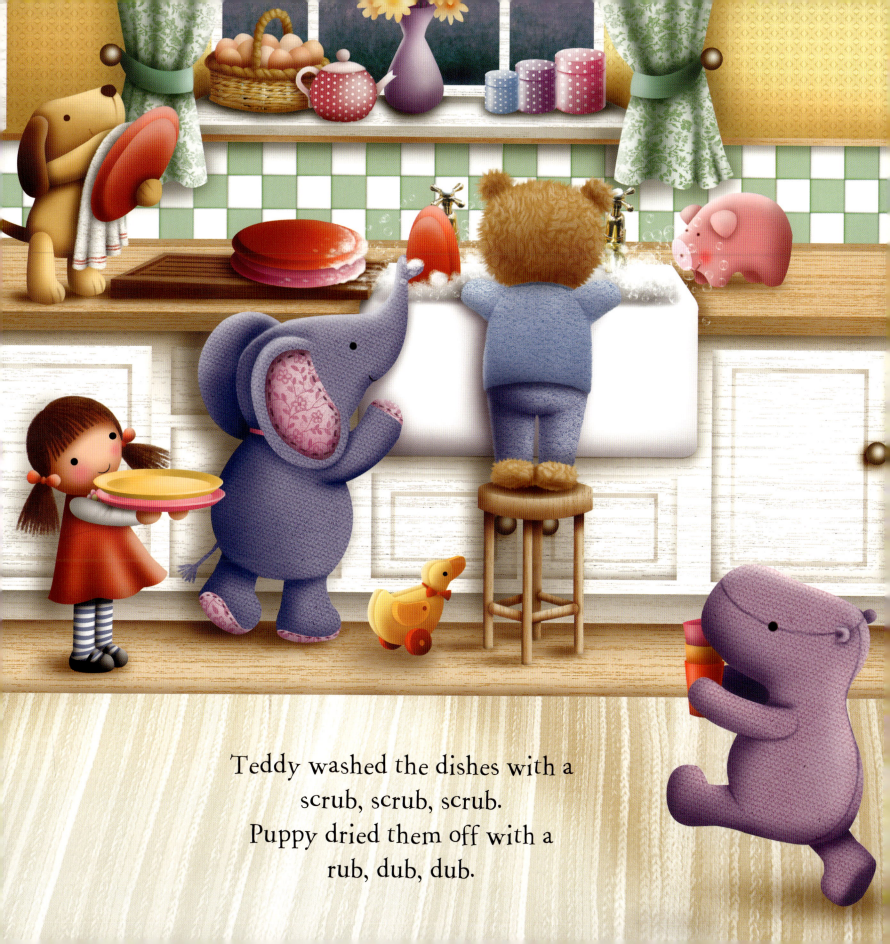

Teddy washed the dishes with a
scrub, scrub, scrub.
Puppy dried them off with a
rub, dub, dub.

Outside, the stars were fading fast
and it was nearly dawn.
"Back to the toybox everyone,"
said Teddy, with a yawn.

Up the stairs, the toys all climbed,
as quickly as they could go.
Teddy felt very sleepy,
his little legs started to slow.

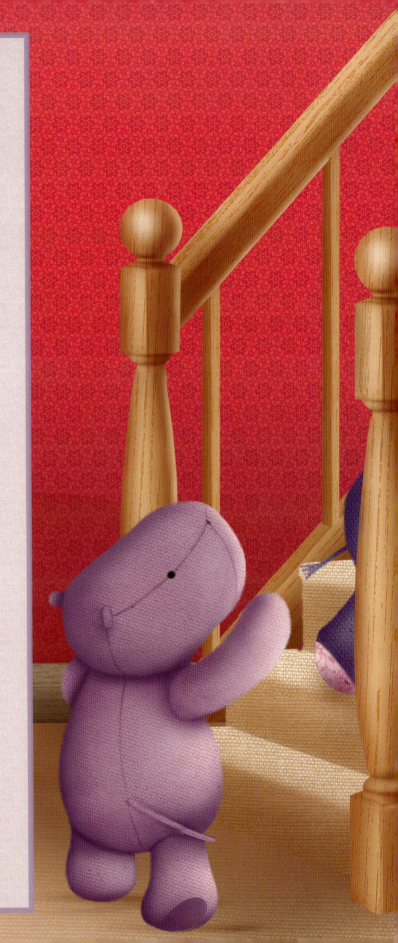

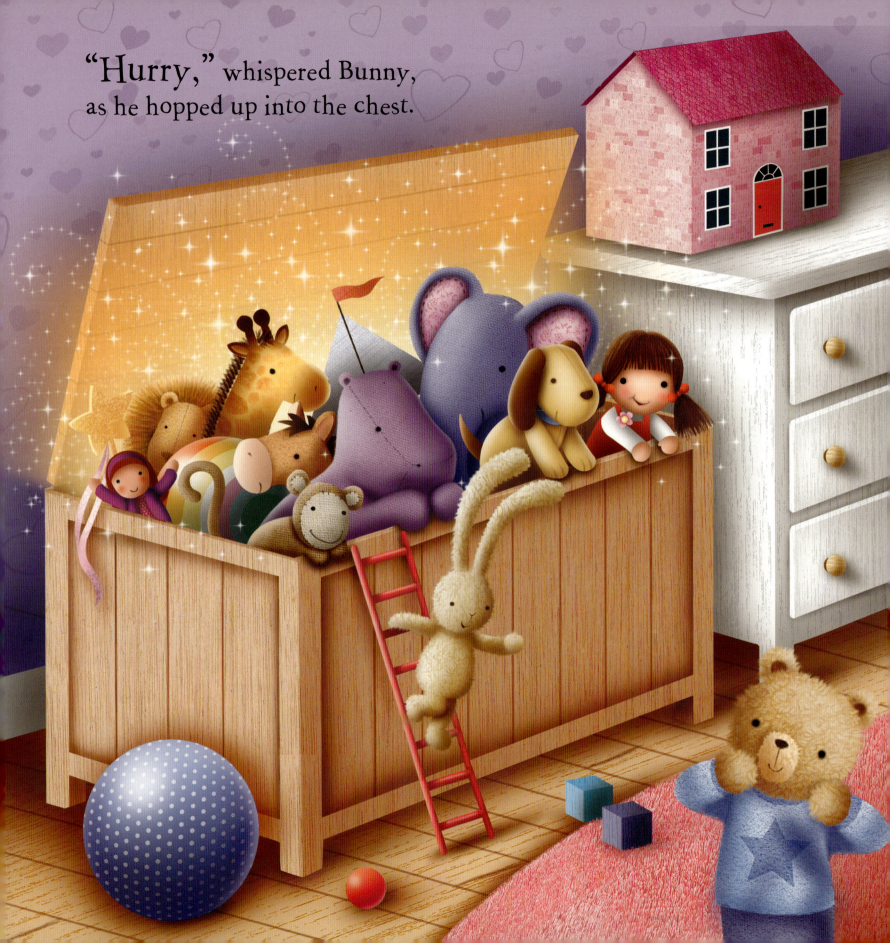

"Hurry," whispered Bunny,
as he hopped up into the chest.

"Hey! Wait for me!" cried Teddy,
who had stopped to take a rest.

The toybox lid was closing,
so Teddy laid on the floor.
Soon, he was in a deep sleep
and softly began to snore.

When morning came, Lucy woke up and shook her sleepy head.
She saw the sunshine streaming in and jumped out of her bed.

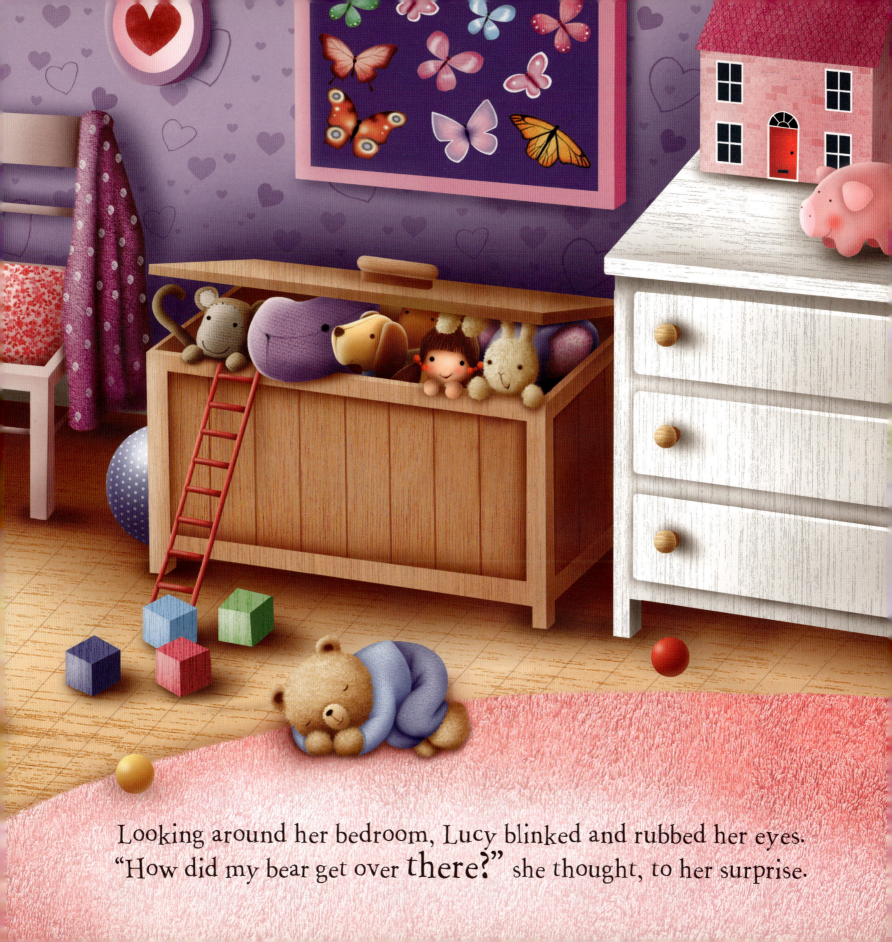

Looking around her bedroom, Lucy blinked and rubbed her eyes.
"How did my bear get over **there?**" she thought, to her surprise.

"Lovely Bear," said Lucy,
as she kissed and cuddled him tight.
"I **wonder** what you were doing,
while I was asleep last night."